George Lambert

The Worshipful Company of Pattenmakers

A list of master, wardens, court of assistants and livery

George Lambert

The Worshipful Company of Pattenmakers
A list of master, wardens, court of assistants and livery

ISBN/EAN: 9783337285159

Printed in Europe, USA, Canada, Australia, Japan

Cover: Foto ©Andreas Hilbeck / pixelio.de

More available books at **www.hansebooks.com**

RECIPIUNT FOEMINÆ SUSTENTACULA NOBIS

THE WORSHIPFUL
COMPANY OF PATTENMAKERS.

─────❦─────

A LIST

OF

MASTER, WARDENS,

COURT OF ASSISTANTS,

AND

LIVERY,

WITH A

"SHORT ACCOUNT OF THE PATTEN,"

AND

"TWO YEARS' IN THE CHAIR,"

By GEORGE LAMBERT, F.S.A.,

Master, 1884—1886.

~~~~~~~~~~

1890.

Master.

HERBERT H. BARTLETT.

Upper Warden.

ALFRED JOSEPH BAKER.

Renter Warden.

PETER TOCHER.

Court of Assistants.

* BARROW EMANUEL, M.A.

* WILLIAM HENRY PANNELL, C.C.

* JAMES ALFRED THORNHILL, F.R.G.S.

** GEORGE LAMBERT, F.S.A.

* RICHARD CLOUT.

* JOHN ALEXANDER BRAND.

* WITHAM M. BYWATER.

HENRY LAWSON HOPKINS.

AUGUSTUS FREDERICK GODSON, M.A., M.P.

AUGUSTUS H. G. HARRIS, L.C.C.

WILLIAM JOSEPH FOSTER, C.C., F.S.A.

CLIFFORD PROBYN, L.C.C.

Clerk.

HENRY FREDERICK YOULE,
GUILDHALL.

Those marked * have served the office of Master.

THE LIVERY.

A.

ABERCROMBIE, JOHN,
  2, King William Street, E.C., and
  Bratten Lodge, Green Lanes, Stoke Newington, N.

B.

BAKER, ALFRED JOSEPH,
  11, Queen Victoria Street, E.C., and
  Harlesden Lodge, Harelsden, Middlesex, N.W.

BARKER, WILLIAM ROBERT,
  143, New Bond Street, W.

BARTLETT, HERBERT HENRY,
    25 and 26, Tredegar Square, Bow, E.,
    City Carlton Club, E.C., and
    The Royal London Yacht Club, Savile Row, W.

BRAND, JOHN ALEXANDER,
    Guildhall, E.C., and
    Avenue Road, Crouch End, Hornsey, N.

BYWATER, WITHAM MATTHEW,
    5, Hanover Square, W.

C.

CARTWRIGHT, SAMUEL,
    10, Basinghall Street, E.C., and
    43, Elmore Street, Islington, N.

CLOUT, RICHARD,
    Brome House, West Malling, Kent.

CLOWES, RICHARD,
    Clayton Wickham, Hassocks, Sussex.

COLLARD, FREDERICK ERNEST WOTTON, L.C.C.,
9, Southwark Street, S.E.,
96, Tyrwhitt Road, Brockley, S.E., and
Canterbury, Kent.

COX, WILLIAM JOHN,
2, Coleman Street, E.C.,
53, Arthur Road, Hornsey Road, N.

E

EMANUEL BARROW, M.A.,
2, Finsbury Circus, E.C.
Thatched House Club, St. James's, S.W., and
36, Orsett Terrace, Hyde Park, W.

F

FOSTER, WILLIAM JOSEPH, C.C., F.S.A.
21, Birchin Lane, Cornhill, E.C., and
42, Hogarth Road, South Kensington, S.W.

FRASER, WILLIAM,
Jeffrey's Square, St. Mary Axe, E.C., and
3, Railway Terrace, Epsom, Surrey.

FRENCH, DAVID,
　51, Crutched Friars, E.C., and
　Beresford Villas, Amhurst Road,
　　　　　　　　　　Hackney Downs, N.E.

G.

GANT, JOHN CASTLE,
　Willow Hyrst, Chiddingley, Sussex.

GODSON, AUGUSTUS FREDERICK, M.A., M.P.,
　2, Pump Court, Temple, E.C., and
　23, Cornwall Gardens, South Kensington, S.W.

GRANTHAM, RICHARD BOXALL,
　Northumberland Chambers,
　　　　　Northumberland Avenue, S.W., and
　14, Randolph Crescent, Clifton Gardens,
　　　　　　　　　　　　Maida Vale, W.

GRAY, ROBERT,
　6, Moorgate Street, E.C., and
　70, Buckleigh Road, Streatham Common, S.W.

GRESHAM, JAMES HAREBOOTH,
　19, Macaulay Road, Clapham, S.W.

H.

HAND, HENRY AUGUSTUS FREDERICK,
74, Bridge Road, Hammersmith, W.

HARRIS, AUGUSTUS HENRY GLOSSOP, L.C.C.,
The Elms, Avenue Road, Regent's Park, N.W.

HAWKINS, ALFRED TEMPLETON, C.C., D.L., J.P.,
22, Budge Row, E.C., and
32, Lee Terrace, Blackheath, Kent, S.E.

HOLLAND, WILLIAM,
23, Park Road, Blackpool, Lancashire.

HOPKINS, HENRY LAWSON,
42, 43, and 44, Houndsditch, E.C., and
Kenley, Surrey.

HUDSON, CHARLES WILLIAM,
Hudson's Buildings, Wilton Road, Pimlico, S.W.;
St. Thomas's Street, Southwark, S.E., and
Brighton, Sussex.

I.

IRONSIDE, WILLIAM,
1, Gresham Buildings, Basinghall Street, E.C., &
Fairleigh, Sutton, Surrey.

J.

JACOB, WILLIAM HEATON,
  Legacy Duty Office, Somerset House, w.c., and
  29, Sinclair Gardens, Kensington, w.

JOURDAIN, NEVILL,
  18, New Bridge Street, Blackfriars, e.c., and
  Fellows Road, South Hampstead, n.w.

K.

KNIGHT, CHARLES FREDERICK, m.d.,
  Sussex House, 341, Brixton Road, s.w.

L.

LAMBERT, Major GEORGE, f.s.a.,
  10, 11, and 12, Coventry Street, Piccadilly, w.

LOVEGROVE, HENRY,
  26, Budge Row, Cannon Street, e.c., and
  Eboracom, Trinity Road, Tulse Hill, s.w.

M.

MARGRETT, EDWARD,
  1, King Street, and
  25, Eldon Square, Reading, Berks.

McKENZIE, ALEXANDER,
  The Warren, Loughton, Essex.

MILLER, ALBERT HINDSON,
  8, Moorgate Street, E.C., and
  Spencer Cottage, Putney, Surrey, S.W.

MURNANE, GEORGE WEBSTER,
  Vestry Hall, St. Martin's Place, W.C., and
  Roselea, Putney Common, S.W.

N.

NORMAN, His Excellency General Sir HENRY
WYLIE, G.C.B., G.C.M.G., C.I.E., Governor of
                          Queensland.
United Service Club, Pall Mall, S.W.

P.

PACKE, GEORGE JAMES,
  64, Welbeck Street, Cavendish Square, w.

PALMER, AUGUSTUS CUFAUDE,
  7, and 8, Railway Approach, London Bridge,
    Southwark, s.e., and
  Manor Villa, Albert Road, Norwood, Surrey, s.e.

PANNELL, WILLIAM HENRY, C.C.,
  Library Chambers, Basinghall Street, e.c., and
  6, Mandeville Street, w.

PARNELL, WILLIAM HENRY,
  90, Tollington Park, Finsbury Park, N.

PEACOCK, THOMAS FRANCIS,
  12, South Square, Gray's Inn, w.c., and
  Fernlea, Sidcup, Kent.

PHILLIPS, LEWIS HENRY, C.C.,
  52, and 53, Newgate Street, e.c., and
  4, Upper Bedford Place, Russell Square, w.c.

POWELL, GEORGE,
  76, Finsbury Pavement, e.c., and
  60, Graham Road, Dalston, e.

PROBYN, Major CLIFFORD, L.C.C.,
55, Grosvenor Street, W.

PULLEY, THOMAS JELL,
10, Grosvenor Road, Westminster, S.W., and
Jesse Terrace, Reading, Berks.

R.

RAIT, LOGAN McCULLOCH,
31, Moorgate Street, E.C., and
Pembroke House, Upper Park Road,
Hampstead, N.W.

RICHARDSON, ERNEST GEORGE,
27, Newgate Street, E.C.,
Receiver and Accountant General's Office,
General Post Office, St. Martin's-le-Grand, and
20, Hermitage Villas, The Vineyard,
Richmond, Surrey.

ROBINSON, EDWARD LEWIS GAVIN, J.P.,
23, Sackville Street, W., and
Poston, Peterchurch, Herefordshire.

S.

SEWELL, Lieut.-Col. THOMAS DAVIES,
Guildhall, E.C.,
29, Grosvenor Road, S.W., and
Junior United Service Club, S.W.

SKINNER, ALFRED ERNEST,
5, Orchard Street, Portman Square, W., and
31, Norfolk Street, Park Lane, W.

SOANES, TEMPLE HILLYARD HICKS,
95, Bishopsgate Street Within, E.C., and
Pembury, Kent.

SPIER, JULIUS,
25, Bedford Place, Russell Square, W.C.

STIEBEL, EDWARD,
Elm Bank, Carlton Road, Putney Hill, S.W.

STONER, WILLIAM EDWARD,
5, and 6, Bucklersbury, E.C., and
19, King Edward Road, Hackney, E.

T.

TERRY, JAMES,
143, Tufnell Park Road, Holloway, N.

TERRY, JOHN, C.C., F.R.G.S.,
31, Milk Street, E.C., and
The Grange Platt, Boro' Green,
Sevenoaks, Kent.

TETLEY, GEORGE,
13, Norfolk Crescent, Hyde Park, W.

THOMPSON, ALFRED,
The Estates Department, South Eastern Railway,
London Bridge, S.E., and
Wychwood, Clarendon Road, Putney, S.W.

THORNHILL, Captain JAMES ALFRED, F.R.G.S.,
London Hospital, Whitechapel, E., and
Bradbourne Villa, Bushey Hill, Camberwell, S.E.

TOCHER, PETER,
West Smithfield, E.C., and
2, Cornwall Terrace, Regent's Park, N.W.

TODD, WILLIAM ANSELL,
The Clock House, Catford Bridge, Kent, S.E., and
Broad Street, Bristol, Gloucestershire.

TWIGG, WILLIAM JAMES,
  West Smithfield, E.C., and
  Croxted House, Croxted Road, Dulwich, S.E.

W.

WADE, CHARLES JOSIAH,
  153, Leadenhall Street, E.C., and
  North Lodge, Queen's Road, Teddington.

WALKER, ROBERT, F.R.I.B.A.,
  27, Garrick Street, W.C., and
  Marquess Road, Canonbury, N.

WALKER, SAMUEL,
  22, Morgate Street, E.C., and
  Woodberry, Sydenham Hill, S.E.

WALLIS, HENRY ELLIS, C.E.,
  34, Drayton Gardens, South Kensington, S.W.

WELFORD, JOHN,
  Elmwood, Harlesden Lane, Harlesden, N.W.

WESTERN, HARRY,
  11, Halkin Street West, Belgrave Square, S.W.

WETENHALL, HENRY HORATIO,
    4, Copthall Buildings, Throgmorton St., E.C., &
    The Limes, Green Lanes, Stoke Newington, N.

WILDASH, FREDERICK CHARLES,
    Comptroller's Office, Guildhall, E.C., and
    33, Stanley Gardens, Haverstock Hill, N.W.

WILKIN, JAMES HARRY,
    47, Kensington Gardens Square, W.

WILLIAMSON, Captain WILLIAM BLIZZARD,
                Alderman and J.P. for Worcester,
    Battenhall, Worcester.

WINK, JOHN ADAM,
    2, Devonshire Square, Bishopsgate, E., and
    Gordon Villa, Claremont Road, Highgate, N.

Y.

YOULE, HENRY FREDERICK,
    Guildhall, E.C., and
    Lion House, Angell Road, Brixton, S.W.

N.B.—It is particularly requested that any change
    of address may be notified to the Clerk.

A SHORT ACCOUNT

OF

THE PATTEN.

ITH respect to coverings for the feet and to guard them from harm "lest Thou dash Thy feet against a stone," Ps. xci. 12, very little can be said, because we are treating about clogs or skates called patins and not about shoes ; but that the Greeks protected the sole of the foot with a flat piece of wood fastened round the angle and leg by a strip of untanned hide, is beyond all doubt "si fides statuis Telamonis Pyrrhi," and Philostratus calls them σανδάλια, a term used in later times by the Romans under the same word *sandaliæ*, or sandals :—

Pythagoras in *Vita Apollonii* (Lib. viii. p. 387) " discipulis calceamenta ex arborum corticibus fieri mandavit : quæ sane materia fragilior esse videbantur, quam ut posset in talem usum assum longe firmior calceorum Empedoclis materia, qui, si fides quibusdam a Strabone allatis ænei toti erant." (Lib. vi. p. 189).

The Romans used various foot-coverings, but only with the " caligæ," the " sandaliæ " and the " soleæ," have we to deal. All three had wooden " soleæ," and hence the word soles, and all were tied on to the foot by bands of tanned leather or raw hide thongs. The shoes of the chiefs of the army and the emperors, were called " campagi," which differed but little from that of the soldier * who, like the legionaries. wore the " caligæ," as is figured upon the columns of Trajan. The flat part under the foot was made of wood, and it was from the thongs that bound the wood to the leg that the Emperor Caius Cæsar (A.D. 37—41) took his name " Caligula," † he having been born in the army, and bred up in the habit of a common soldier, and hence his troops were called "Caligati" (Suetonius *Calig.* Chap. ix.)

---

* " Imperatorum Ducum Tribunorumque exercitus calceamentum campagus vocabatur parumque a caligis militum differebat."—*Montfaucon*, tome v., p. 219.

† A harness for the legs set full of nails used by soldiers, especially of the common sort in the Roman army.

The sandals, "caligæ," and the campagi, covered
only the flat of the foot with a sole of leather or
wood, to which was attached bands of leather,
which crossed the top of the foot, leaving an
interval here and there to show the naked flesh,
but so little and few passages occur in the ancient
writers to explain this mode of protecting the foot,
that it is impossible to discover the changes which
came into use from time to time, or even the form
and denomination of them. Cicero mentions in
two places that "soleæ," or soles, were made of
wood, and that they were applied to the feet of
criminals when going to prison, but taken off on
their arrival there.*

It has been said "that Mercury was the first
maker of skates, and that the wings upon his feet
are the symbols of the invention." (S. T. Coleridge).

Strutt, in his *Sports and Pastimes*, confesses his
inability to trace the introduction of skating into

---

* " Ez iis quæ Cicero bis ait de inventione (b. 2) liquet soleas
illas ligneas aliquando fuisse, cujusmodi solea reorum pedibus
admovebantur. Quidam (inquit) judicatus est parentem
occidisse et statim, quod effugiendi potestas non fuit, ligneæ
soleæ in pedes inductæ sunt. . . . Deinde est in carcerem
deductus."

this country; and it would be very difficult to
fix any correct date, for we are constantly finding
below the level of the surface of the north-eastern
and eastern parts of London (which it is well
known was a swamp), skates made of the bones
of sheep and other beasts, which, according to
Fitz-Stephen, who lived in the time of Henry II.,
1154—1188, "they placed under the soles of their
feet by tying round their ankles, and then, taking
a pole, shod with iron, into their hands, they push
themselves forward by striking it against the ice,
and are carried on with a velocity equal to the
flight of a bird, or a bolt discharged from a cross-
bow."

In 1841, February 18, Mr. Charles Roach Smith
exhihited to the Society of Antiquaries an ancient
bone skate. "It was formed of the bone of some
animal made smooth on one side, with a hole at
one extremity for a cord to fasten it to the shoe.
At the other end a hole was also drilled horizontally
to the depth of three inches, which was to receive
a plug, with another cord to secure it more
effectually." It was found in Moorfields, near
Finsbury Circus in the boggy soil peculiar to that
district.

Later on they wore wooden skates shod with

iron, and bound about the feet and legs with straps like the talares of the Greeks and sandals of the Romans. These seem to have been introduced into England from the Low Countries, where during the winter season skates are the only means of "circulation" (getting about), and are used by both sexes.

Fosbroke, in his *Dictionary of Antiquities*, says:— "The Icelanders also used the shankbone of a deer or sheep about a foot long, which they grease, because that they should not be stopped by drops of water upon them."

In Danish the word for skate is "schaats"* and is described as a framework of wood furnished with a smooth iron; this is fastened under the foot for moving rapidly on the ice.

> "He smote the sledded Polacks on the Ice."
>
> *Hamlet*, Act I, Scene i.

In the translation of Runic poetry by Bishop Percy from the Icelandic language (London, 1763), skating is alluded to as one of the accomplish-

---

* Skate in Dutch, "schætsen," which is the derivation of the English word. *Vlæmisch Dictionary*, 1699.

ments of the north. Harold, in the poem called
His Complaint, says : " I glide along the ice on
scates, ... and yet a Russian maid
disdains me."

In the 24th table of the *Edda,* skating is spoken
of thus :—

" Then the King asked what that young man
could do who accompanied Thor. Thialfe answered
' that in running upon scates he would dispute the
prize with any of the countries,' whereupon the
King said he owned the talent was great, a very
fine one." *

Now if there may arise any question among
Runic scholars, as to whether the above passage
refers to the traversing the snow on skates of wood,
Olous Magnusk agrees perfectly with Fitz-Stephen,
for he speaks of it as being of polished iron, or of
the shank-bone of a deer or sheep a foot long,
filed down on one side and greased with hog's lard
to repel the wet.

" Aliud vero genus quod ferro plano et polito
sive planis ossibus, cervinus vel bovinis scilicet
tibiis, naturalem lubricitatem ob innatum pingue-

---

* Mallet's *Introduction à l'Histoire de Danemarc*, vol. ii., 1770.

dinem habentibus, pedali longitudine sub plantis
affixis, in sola glacie lubrica cursum indendit
velocissimum; quemque in glaciali æqualitate
semper currendo continuat. Cæteris bravium
lucraturi currendo præveniunt, qui cervinas tibias
latè limatas plantis affigunt, porcina, axungia
perunctas, quia gelidis æquæ guttis velut per
poros glaciei in vehementi frigore surgentibus
tibiæ sic unctæ impediri aut constringi non
possunt.—" Hist. Olai Magni de Gent. Sep-
tentrion." Basileæ. *Archæologia*, vol. xxix. pp.
397, 398.

It is believed that the name of patten comes
from the French *pattin* or *patin*, for in England in
early times, French or Norman French was as much
spoken as English, and the word patin was applied
to the skate. It was used thus: *patin de femme*
a clog—and patin also serves to denote a horseshoe
sorte de fer de cheval (Boyer's Dictionary, 1727).
In Gruë's Dutch Dictionary (Amsterdam, 1699)
patins or skates are called *schaetsen*, to run upon
the ice. A better explanation than from the
clumsy iron-shod clog, worn by women during the
last century and well into the middle of this.
This view is somewhat supported by a paragraph
in the *Gentleman's Magazine*, 1789, in which it

states that " Crupers were a sort of patten, having
three knobs of iron instead of the ring still in use."
Old Pepys says skating was introduced by Cavaliers
who had been with Charles II. in Holland, in
vol. ii., page 73, under the date of December 1st,
1662 : " To the Parke, where I first in my life, it
being a greate frost, did see people sliding with
skates, which is a very pretty art." Mr. Evelyn
mentions in his Diary on this very December 1st,
1662, how he " Went to the park to see the
dexterity of the sliders on the new canal in
St. James's, with what swiftness they pass with
skates after the manner of the Hollanders ; how
suddenly they can stop in full career upon the
ice."

Lines under an Old Engraving.

" Sur un mince chyrstal l'hiver conduit leur pas,
   Le précipice est sous la glace,
   Telle est de nos plaisirs la légère surface
   Glissez mortels ; n'appuyez pas."

" O'er the ice the rapid skater flies,
   With sport above and Death below,
   Where mischief lurks in gay disguise,
   Thus lightly touch and quickly go."

                    Translated by Dr. JOHNSON (?).

Notes and Queries, Series ii., vol. ii., p. 508.

"In frosty season when the sun
Was set and visible for many a mile"

*   *   *   *   *

"I wheel'd about,
Proud and exulting, like an untired horse
That cared not for its home. All shod with steel
We hissed along the polished ice in games
Confederate, imitative of the chase."

*   *   *   *   *

"Not seldom from the uproar I retired
Into a silent bay, or sportively
Glanced sideway, leaving the tumultuous throng,
To cut across the image of a star
That gleamed upon the ice. And oftentimes
When we had given our bodies to the wind,
And all the shadowy banks on either side
Came sweeping through the darkness, shunning still
The rapid line of motion, then at once
Have I, reclining back upon my heels,
Stopped short."

WORDSWORTH.

Pattens and clogs were anciently worn by persons of quality as well as others, and the makers of them were an ancient company, and there is a parish church in London, called from them, St. Margaret Pattens, those of the trade of Pattenmakers having their stalls or shops set up in the immediate precincts of that church. In an Act of 4 of Edward IV. they are called the "Mysterie of the Pattenmakers," &c. They

made a complaint to the King asking for an Act
of Parliament, and they obtained it, in their behalf,
upon a complaint which they made of the grievous
hurt and damage which they and other persons in
time past, of the same occupation, had suffered by
an Act of Parliament, 4 of Henry V., that abridged
them of the using of timber of " asp " in making
pattens and clogs upon a penalty for the benefit of
the fletchers who used that wood, that they might
sell their shafts at easier prices. But they showed
how that this wood was the best and lightest
timber for pattens and clogs and most easy for the
wearing of all estates, gentlemen and other people
and that persons of other crafts and occupations,
as turners, carpenters, woodmongers, and coal
(charcoal makers), used this wood and had no
restraint put upon them ; and that there was
much asp-timber, and fit for the fletchers' use to
make shafts, which they, the Pattenmakers, could
not use, but which they, the fletchers, should use;
whereupon the Parliament enacted that it should
be lawful from henceforth, that the Pattenmakers
might make pattens of such timber of asp, as was
not apt nor convenient to be made into shafts * or

* *Strype upon Stowe*, Ed. 1755, vol. ii., book v., page 328.

arrows; wherefore upon this showing, the Act
was granted to them conferring on them all the
benefits that they desired.

The poltine or poltint was called a patten; it
was a sort of shoe, sharped or pricked, and turned
up at the toe. They first came into fashion in the
reign of William Rufus, and by degrees came to
be of such excessive length, that in Richard II.'s
time they were tied up to the knees with chains of
silver and gold, according to the dignity of the
wearer. They were forbidden by Edward IV. in
the fifth year of his reign, under a penalty, to be
worn so long, but were not utterly laid aside till
the reign of Henry VIII. William of Malmes-
bury speaking of the excesses of those times,
hath these words: " Tunc fluxus crinium, tunc
luxus vestium—tunc usus calceorum cum arcuatis
aculeis inventus est."

Speaking of clogs or pattens, Shakspere in
Hamlet, Prince of Denmark, says:—"By'r lady,
your ladyship is nearer heaven, than when I saw
you last, by the altitude of a 'chopine,'" and the
best description of them is to be found in Coryat's
Crodilies, published in 1611. Mr. Evelyn, writing
in 1645, says:—" It is now Ascension week. . . .
the noblemen stalking with their ladies on ' chop-

pines,' . . . . it is ridiculous to see how these ladies crawl in and out of their gondolas by reason of these choppines, and what dwarfs they appear when taken down from their wooden scaffolds. They wear things made of wood, covered with leather of sundry colours, white, red, yellow ; they are called ' chapineys,' which they wear under the soles of their shoes. Some are painted, some I have seen fairly gilt ; they are such uncomely things that it is a pity that this foolish custom is not banished and exterminated out of the city (Venice). There are many of these chapineys of a great height, even to half a yard high. A person was once asked ' how he liked the Venetian ladies ; ' he replied, they were ' Mezzo carne, mezzo legno,' half flesh, half wood. The wives or widows of wealthy gentlemen are supported on either side by men or women servants when they walk abroad to the end that they may not fall, and they are borne up mostly by the left arm." The old patten was shaped like the more modern clog. The ringed patten is not older than the time of Anne.

"The tongue runs on pattens," was a saying of the sixteenth century, to denote garrulity.

> " Had ye heard her, how she begun to scold,
>   The tongue it were on pattens."
>
>   *Gammer Girton's Needle.*

Dickens, in his *Cricket on the Hearth*, page 3, says :—" Mrs. Peerybingle going out into the raw twilight, and clicking over the wet stones in a pair of pattens that worked innumerable rough impressions of the first proposition in Euclid all about the yard. That pattens were difficult to walk in is shown by the fact that Mrs. Peerybingle returned without the pattens, for they were tall, while Mrs. P. was but short, for the water being cold, and in that slippy, slushy, sleety, sort of state, wherein it seemed to penetrate through every substance, patten rings included."

Gay, in his *Trivia, or The Art of Walking the Streets of London*, writes :—

> " Good housewives all the winter's rage despise,
>   Defended by the riding-hood's disguise ;
>   Or underneath th' umbrella's oily shed
>   Safe through the wet, on clinking pattens tread.
>   But O ! forget not, Muse, the Patten's praise,
>   That female implement shall grace thy lays ;
>   Say from what art divine th' invention came
>   And from its origin deduce its name.
>   Where Lincoln wide extends her fenny soil
>   A goodly Yeoman lived, grown white with toil ;
>   One only daughter blest his nuptial bed

Who from her infant hand the poultry fed.
Martha (her careful mother's name) she bore,
But now her careful mother was no more !
Whilst on her father's knee the damsel played,
Patty he fondly called the smiling maid.
As years increased, her ruddy beauty grew,
And Patty's fame o'er all the village flew.
Soon as the grey-eyed morning streaks the skies,
And in the doubtful day the woodcock flies,
Her cleanly pail the pretty housewife bears,
And singing, to the distant field repairs ;
And when the plains with evening dews are spread,
The milky burthen smoaks upon her head.
Deep through a miry lane she picked her way,
Above her ankle rose the chalky clay.
Vulcan by chance the bloomy maiden spies,
With innocence and beauty in her eyes ;
He saw, he loved : for yet he ne'er had known
Sweet innocence and beauty met in one.
Ah, Mulciber ! I recall thy nuptial vows,
Think on the graces of thy Paphian spouse ;
Think how her eyes dart inexhausted charms,
And canst thou leave her bed for Patty's arms ?
The Lemnian Power forsakes the realms above,
His bosom glowing with terrestrial love ;
Far in the lane a lonely hut he found,
No tenant ventured on the unwholesome ground.
Here smokes his forge, he bares his sinewy arm,
And early strokes the sounding anvil warm ;
Around his shop the steely sparkles flew,
And for the steed he shaped the bending shoe.
When blue-eyed Patty near his window came,
His anvil rests, his forge forgets to flame ;
To hear his soothing tales she feigns delays,

What woman can resist the face of praise ?
At first, she coyly every kiss withstood,
And all her cheek was flushed with modest blood ;
With headless nails he now surrounds her shoes,
To save her steps from rains and piercing dews.
She liked his soothing tales, his presents wore,
And granted kisses, but would grant no more.
Yet winter chilled her feet, with cold she pines,
And on her cheek the fading rose declines,
No more her humid eyes their lustre boast,
And, in hoarse sounds, her melting voice is lost.
This Vulcan saw, and in his heavenly thought,
A new machine mechanic, fancy wrought,
Above the mire her shelter'd steps to raise,
And bear her safely through the wintry ways ;
Strait the new engine on his anvil glows,
And the pale virgin on the PATTEN rose.
No more her lungs are shook with drooping rheums,
And on her cheek reviving beauty blooms ;
The god obtained his suit: though flattery fail,
Presents with female virtue must prevail.
The Patten now supports each frugal dame,
Which from the blue-eyed Patty takes the name."

GAY'S *Trivia*, book i., line 202 to 282.

The Pattenmakers' Company was incorporated
by Charles II. in 1670. By their charter, all
persons using the art or mystery of making pattens
or clogs within the cities of London and Westminster, and ten miles every way distant therefrom,
are incorporated by the name of the Master,
Wardens, Assistants and Fellowship of the

Company of Pattenmakers of the City of London, with power to make bye-laws for the government of its own members, and for the regulation of the trade, and to impose fines and amercements for offences against such bye-laws.

The Court of Aldermen, by an order dated 1674, decree that all persons using the trade of Patten-makers are to be admitted into the freedom of the city in that city only.

The Company's bye-laws were made on the 27th of October, 1673, under the provisions of an Act, 19 Henry VII.

The effect of the bye-laws is to regulate the estate, rule and government of the Fellowship, and the members thereof, and in what manner the Company and all persons using or exercising the art and mystery of making pattens and clogs within the cities of London and Westminster, and ten miles every way distant therefrom, shall demean and behave themselves as well in all matters touching and concerning the trade, as in their offices, functions, places and businesses touching or concerning the Company.

These bye-laws were approved by Sir HENEAGE FINCH, Bart., Lord Chancellor Sir MATTHEW HALE, Knight, and Sir JOHN VAUGHAN, Knight, the

Lords Justices of the Courts of King's Bench, and the Common Pleas, dated June 20, in the twenty-sixth year of the reign of Charles II. 1674.

The Company is the 76th of the 89 Companies of London ; it has a Livery as before set out, but no Hall.

EXTRACT FROM

MR. SCRIMSHAW'S BEQUEST.

THE late MR. THOMAS SCRIMSHAW, by his Will, left, after the decease of his . will, the interest of £1000 in the Three per Cent. Government Securities, being £30 per annum to the PATTENMAKERS' COMPANY in trust as under :—

£500 part thereof, to defray the expenses against all unlawful workers; and if that should not be wanted to pay for a march and dinner once in three years, on the Lord Mayor's Day (9th November) for ever: and £500, the remainder, that they should, every year, for ever, give or pay unto four poor men, free of the said Company, and working Pattenmakers, and free of the City of London, or to the widows of the aforesaid four such Pattenmakers, 40s. each per annum, being £8, and the remainder (£7 per annum) to pay for a dinner every year, for ever, for the Court, of Assistants on the election day for Master and Wardens; and on that day to pay the aforesaid £8 to the aforesaid poor people, either men or women, as above named, for ever.

CHARGES AND EXPENSES UPON BINDING
APPRENTICES AND ADMISSION TO THE FREEDOM
AND LIVERY.

Bindings, exclusive of Stamp £ s. d.
  Duty, which is governed
  by the amount of Premium 1 13 6
Admission to the Freedom by £ s. d.
  Patrimony or Servitude . 1 17 6
  Stamp Duty 1 0 0
              ————— 2 17 0
Admission to ditto by Redemption 9 18 6
  Stamp Duty. 3 0 0
             ————— 12 8 6
Admission to the Livery,
  including £2 for the
  redemption of Quarterage . . . 15 0 0

The Admission to the Court is a fee or fine of
£50.

The governing body of Master, Wardens, and
Assistants, are paid 10s. each for their attendance
at the four Quarterly Courts of the Company.
Non-Attendants are fined 5s. to be put into the
poor box, to be annually divided, with the other
sums, among the Company's poor.

Parties can be bound and admitted to the Freedom and Livery on application to Mr. YOULE, the Clerk of the Company, at Guildhall, any day, Sundays excepted, between the hours of Eleven and Three.

GEORGE LAMBERT,

10, 11, & 12, *Coventry Street,*

London, W.

𝕸𝖆𝖘𝖙𝖊𝖗, 1884·5.

TWO YEARS' WORK IN THE CHAIR

OF THE

PATTENMAKERS,

1884—1886.

ASSUMED the Chair of the Pattenmakers, Thursday, March 20th, 1884, and adjourned to the "Guildhall Tavern," where a select dinner was held.

On the 24th April the new Master gave his Inauguration Dinner at the "Holborn Restaurant," at which the Lord Mayor, Sir Nicholas R. Fowler— (who came late from the House of Commons)—and the Sheriffs, Messrs. Faudel Phillips, and Mr. Alderman Whitehead, supported by 170 gentlemen of the Court and Livery and general visitors, including Admiral Stopford, Sir E. Lechmere, M.P., Major-General Milman, the Hon. S. A. Joseph, Member of the Upper House of Legislature of New South Wales, and several Masters of City Companies were present.

On the 29th April, the Master of the Patten-makers took his seat as the President of the City Waiters' Pension and Provident Institution, that office having been most generously surrendered by Sir John Bennett.

On the 30th April, the Master dined, by the kind invitation of the Lord Mayor, at the Mansion House, with the Masters of other City Companies.

On the 8th May he attended at the Health Exhibition, South Kensington, to meet His Royal Highness the Prince of Wales, who had graciously consented to open the Exhibition. The Master took up his position at the door of the Patten-makers' Shop, which, by the untiring energy of Mr. Warden Brand (the Comptroller of the Chamber of London), had been supplied with a collection of Clogs, Shoes, and Pattens, which Exhibition was not equalled by any other Shop in the Old London Section.

The Master of the Pattenmakers' Company, having been appointed .Chairman of the Jury for awarding prizes and judging the Works in Horn, by the Worshipful Company of Horners, dined with that Company, on the 19th May, and received his instructions from their Master and Clerk.

On the 9th June, the Master and Wardens

entertained at the "Holborn Restaurant" the Honourable and Learned Societies of London, notably the Royal Society of London, represented by Sir Frederick Bramwell, John Evans, Esq., LL.D., Jas. Glashier, Esq. (of balloon celebrity), and others ; the Antiquaries, the Deputy-Master of the Royal Mint, the British Archæological Association, the Royal Archæological Institute, the British Association, the London and Middlesex Archæological Association, the Numismatic Society, Officers of the Navy, Army, and Volunteers, and several Members of the House of Commons.

On the 11th June the Master dined with the Honourable the Traders' Society.

On the 20th June, he dined with the Glass Sellers' Company at the "Ship Tavern," Greenwich.

On the 21st June, the Master, having received a very polite invitation from Frederick Gordon, Esq., of Bentley Priory, near Bushey, Herts, attended at a magnificent *fête champêtre* and public breakfast.

On Monday 23rd June, he was present at a banquet of the Needlemakers' Company, at the "Albion Tavern," Aldersgate Street.

On the 26th June the Master dined by invitation of the Worshipful the Armourers' and Braziers'

Company at their splendid hall in Coleman Street, where he had the honour of returning thanks for the City Companies, particularly the Pattenmakers' and the Goldsmiths', of which he was a Warden.

On July 2nd, 1884, the Master had the honour to preside over a dinner given by the Royal Gardeners' Benevolent Institution, at the " Albion Tavern," Aldersgate Street, to which 180 gentlemen—French, Belgian, Dutch, and English—sat down ; and the subscription exceeded any that had been collected before, although Royalty and other notabilities had taken the chair. The Pattenmakers are now Life Governors of that Charity.

On the 3rd July, the Master of the Pattenmakers having accepted the polite invitation of the Worshipful the Curriers' Company, dined at the " Star and Garter " at Richmond.

On the 10th of July, he had the honour of dining with the Vintners' Company, and returned thanks for the Army, Navy, and Reserve forces.

On the 19th July, he presided at the Annual Festival of the Dressing Case Makers' and Fancy Leather Goods Makers' Benevolent and Provident Iustitution (which Institution rejoiced, if they got a collection of £50), now netted a subscription of just under £400.

On the 23rd of July, at the "New Falcon" Hotel, Gravesend, the Master of the Pattenmakers' Company entertained the Wardens and the Members of the Court and their Ladies, and the Master and their Ladies, of six of the City Companies.

After this the Master had two months' repose, until the 16th October, 1884, when he invited the Court and their Ladies to meet him, and dine at the Holborn Restaurant, when some American ladies and gentlemen formed part of the Company. Mr. Delille, the representative of the *American Register* (newspaper), returned thanks for their kind reception.

On the 7th November, the Master of the Pattenmakers was duly elected a Member of the Court of the Gold and Silver Wyre Drawers' Company of London, and subscribed his declaration accordingly.

On the 21st November, he had the honour of dining at a banquet of the Cutlers' Company.

On the 26th November, the Master of the Pattenmakers had the honour to represent his Company at a grand dinner, given by the Worshipful the Turners' Company, and returned thanks in the name of his Company for the favour thus conferred.

On the 10th December the Master represented
the Company at the Honourable the Traders'
Society, and this last dinner brought the year
1884 to a close.

1885.

The first dinner of the year, was held January
15th, at the " Ship and Turtle Tavern," where the
Master of the Pattenmakers' Company entertained the gentleman of the Court and a few
friends.

The Masters and Wardens of the Worshipful
Company of Fruiterers kindly sent an invitation
for the Master to dine at the "Albion" to
H. F. Youle, Esq., the Clerk, which the Master,
in obedience to the polite summons, accepted, and
after the dinner, returned thanks for the toast of
the City Companies, and, prior to resuming his
seat, proposed the toast of the Master and
Wardens of the Fruiterers' Company.

On the 20th February the Master had the
honour to receive an invitation (sent to the Clerk
of the Company, H. F. Youle, Esq.) to dine with
the Spectaclemakers' Company, where he returned thanks for the Reserve Forces, the Master

of the Pattenmakers' Company being a Captain in the Queen's Westminster Volunteers.

On the 18th March he had the honour of dining with the Glass Sellers' Company, and responded on behalf of the Lord Mayor, Mr. Alderman Nottage, the Sheriffs and the Corporation of the City of London.

On the 19th March, the Master had the unparalleled honour conferred upon him of being elected for the second time Master of the Pattenmakers' Company, to which he demurred—nay, even objected; but, being overruled by the members of the Court, he submitted; and afterwards the Master of the Company, by the permission of the Wardens, entertained a brilliant company of 188 gentlemen to dinner in the Venetian Saloon at the Holborn Restaurant, amongst whom were the Lord Mayor, Sheriffs and Under-Sheriffs, Alderman Sir Robert Carden, Alderman Savory, Sir W. Charley, Q.C., The Prime-Warden of the Goldsmiths' Company, the Masters of fourteen of the City Companies, F. H. Fowler, Esq., Deputy-Chairman of the Metropolitan Board of Works.

On the 25th March the Master of the Company presided over a banquet given on behalf of the

United Waiters of London, Westminster, and
Brighton, the subscription amounting to £108,
ably and most kindly added to by Colonel Peters
and Frederick Binckes, Esq.. who not being themselves " United Waiters," yet, hearing that the
Master of the Pattenmakers' Company was in the
Chair, brought up the subscription some £30,
besides their very handsome and liberal donations.

April 1st, the Master had the honour of dining
at the New Hall of the Leathersellers', and
gratefully acknowledged the toast of the Visitors.

On the 10th April. he partook of the kind
hospitality of the Wheelwrights' Company, and
acknowledged the toast of the Reserve Forces.

It was on Saturday night, April 11th, that the
lamented death of the Right. Hon. the Lord
Mayor, Mr. Alderman Nottage, occurred, and cast
a gloom over the city; and on the following
Sunday the Master of the Pattenmakers left his
card at the Mansion House, being one of the first
callers to show to Mrs. Nottage and family that
respect which was felt for the illustrious deceased
citizen, who, only a few days prior to the awful
event had invited the Master of the Pattenmakers
to be present at the Reception of the Lady
Mayoress. The Master attended in his robes the

State Funeral of the late Lord Mayor at St. Paul's Cathedral.

On Wednesday, the 22nd April, he had the honour of dining with the Cooks' Company, and proposed the health of the Master of that Company.

On the 23rd the Master having accepted the invitation to dine with the Girdlers' Company, responded to the toast of the Navy, the Army, and Reserve Forces.

On the 30th, he was entertained at a banquet given by the Needlemakers' Company at the "Albion Tavern," Aldersgate Street.

On the 14th of May, the Court of the Pattenmakers dined together, and entertained visitors.

On Thursday, the 19th May, the Master, as President of the City Waiters, supported the Honourable Member for Brighton, W. T. Marriott, Esq., Q.C., M.P., who took the Chair at the Guildhall Tavern on behalf of that excellent Charity.

On the 2nd of June, the Master dined with the Worshipful the Carpenters' Company at their New Hall, and had the honour to return thanks on behalf of the Visitors.

On the 4th he, having been favoured by an invitation from A. F. Godson, Esq., dined with the Worcestershire Society.

Also on the 9th, at the instance of the Master and Wardens of the Curriers' Company dined at their New Hall in London Wall.

The Worshipful Company of Tin-Plate Workers invited him to dine at the "Albion" on the 30th of June, and, in obedience to the summons, he attended, and was very elegantly entertained, returning thanks for the Reserve Forces and Volunteers.

On the 1st of July, the Master was honoured by an invitation to dine at the Mansion House at the invitation of the Lord Mayor, R. N. Fowler, Esq., M.P.

On the 3rd, he attended a dinner of the Gardeners' Benevolent Institution to support Edward Tidswell, Esq., in the Chair, and had the honour to return thanks for the toast of the Lord Mayor, Sheriffs, and Corporation of the City of London.

On the 6th, the Master was favoured by an invitation to dine at the Drapers' Hall, which had been most kindly placed at the disposal of the Worshipful Company of Fanmakers, and had the honour conferred upon him of speaking on behalf of the Reserve Forces.

On the 9th July, after a Court of Pattenmakers,

the Master and Wardens had the honour to entertain the Members of the Court and their Ladies at
a small dinner at the " Holborn Restaurant."
On Friday, the 10th, he was invited to a dinner
with the Union Society of St. James', held at the
" Trafalgar Hotel," Greenwich, which he attended,
together with his Ladies, (who were invited to
attend,) and returned thanks for the Navy, Army,
and Volunteers.

Saturday, 19th September, the Master of the
Pattenmakers had the honour to entertain the
Wardens, their Ladies, and a select party of
Masters of City Companies and their Ladies at the
" New Falcon Hotel," Gravesend, at a small return
Dinner, for favours already received.

On the 15th October, he had the honour to entertain the Members of the Court and many friends,
together with their Ladies, in the New Rooms at
the " Holborn Restaurant," several Masters of City
Companies and their Ladies being present, to
whom Mr. Hamp, the respected manager and
partner, presented bouquets on leaving.

On the 9th November, the Master of the Patten-
makers attended at the office of Wynne Baxter,
Esq., Laurence Pountney Hill, to take part in the
Procession of the Lord Mayor, Mr. Alderman

Staples, by the courtesy of the Gold and Silver Wyredrawers' Company, who were graciously pleased to give him a seat in a carriage. He had the honour of being invited to lunch with the High Officials in a private room of the Royal Courts of Justice, and by this delay very nearly missed his carriage, which was driving off as the Master reached the entrance-hall in the Strand. On returning to the Guildhall and alighting, got into conversation with William Holland, Esq., one of the Pattenmakers' Company, whereupon, being informed by one of the officials that if the Master was going home to dress, he had no time to lose, so he returned home, but was too tired to go back to the Guildhall, so did not dine there, but later in the evening put in his appearance.

On the 25th November, the Master, having been honoured by an invitation to dine with the Worshipful Drapers' Company, had the honour to propose the Health of the Master, George Lawford, Esq., and this dinner brought the labours of the year 1885 to a close.

1886.

On Thursday, 14th January, the Master gave his last and Farewell Dinner to gentlemen of the Army

and Navy, the Lord Mayor, Mr. Sheriff Clarke, the
Deputy-Master of the Mint, Colonel Howard
Vincent, C.B., M.P. for Sheffield (his Colonel),
twenty-two Masters of the City Companies—viz. :
The Prime Warden and Wardens of the Gold-
smiths' Company.

The Master of the Drapers' Company.

,,	,,	Cutlers' Company.
,,	,,	Tallow Chandlers' Company.
,,	,,	Girdlers' Company.
,,	,,	Butchers' Comgany.
	,,	Carpenters' Company.
,	,,	Curriers' Company.
,,	,,	Founders' Company.
,,	,,	Cooks' Company.
,,	,,	Loriners' Company.
,,	,,	Spectaclemakers' Company.
,,	,,	Clockmakers' Company.
,,	,,	Tinplate Workers' Company.
,,	,,	Wheelwrights' Company.
,,	,,	Glass Sellers' Company.
,	,,	Wyredrawers' Company.
,,	,,	Playing-Cardmakers' Company.
,,	,,	Horners' Company.

And the Clerks of their respective Companies.
The Right Hon. the Lord Mayor, Alderman

Staples, the Sheriffs, Alderman Savory, the Under-Sheriffs, the Town Clerk, L. H. Phillips, Esq., C.C., and C. D. Miller, Esq., C.C., representing the Corporation of the City of London. Admirals Sir William Hewett, K.C.B., and Sir Henry Keppell, G.C.B., Admiral of the Fleet, General Gipps, Sir CharlesWarren, Col. Duncan, M.P., Col. Moncrieff, Sir James McGarel Hogg, Bart, M.P., Col. Shadwell H. Clerke, Col. Mahon, Capt. Phillips, Col. Lynch, Col. J. Davis, Col. Harding, Col. Shipway, Major Mends, Major Roper D. Tyler, Major McKenzie, Capt. C. Probyn, Capt. H. Scrivener, Capt. Bowyer, Lieut. H. C. Lambert, The Hon. C. Fremantle, The Mayor of Reigate, F. H. Philbrick, Esq., Q.C., Rev. Dr. Maguire, Rev. J. H. Rose, M.A., A. White, Esq., F.S.A , W. Brabrook, Esq., F.S.A., G. R. Wright, Esq., F.S.A., W. J. Foster, Esq., F.R.G.S., Dr. Cowell, Dr. Cross, Dr. Mickley, Dr. Swaine, Dr. R. Graves Burton, Dr. C. F. Knight, Dr. Arthur Cross, who, with other gentlemen, representing many of the learned societies of London (except the Antiquaries, which had a meeting on the same night, and were not present—yet represented by some of the Fellows) and numbering 238 guests sat down under the Master's presidency.

On the 25th January, the Master was honoured
with an invitation to the Consecration of the Drury
Lane Lodge, but was unable to attend, having to
attend the banquet of the Fruiterers' Company to
meet the Lord Mayor, the Right Hon. John
Staples, and the Sheriffs at the " Albion."

On the 27th, the Master was invited by the
Lodge of Antiquity which he attended.

On the 4th of February, the Master was invited
by Deputy Master Benjamin Venables to dine with
the Butchers' Company, when he had the honour
responding for the Army, Navy, and Reserve
Forces.

On the 6th March, the Master had the honour of
an invitation to dine with the Fanmakers' Company at Drapers' Hall, which, by the courtesy of
the Master, G. Lawford, Esq., and the Wardens,
had been lent to the Fanmakers for the occasion,
and he returned thanks for the Reserve Forces.

This last dinner brought the labours of the
Master to an end, and he feels bound to return
his best and most grateful thanks to the Masters
of City Companies, who have honoured the Worshipful Company of Pattenmakers, in the person
of the Master, with a round of invitations, almost
unprecedented in the annals of the Pattenmakers

Company. And the Master earnestly hopes that the gentlemen who are now about to assume the chair (which he vacates) will not lose the opportunity to keep the Pattenmakers as prominently before the public and the City as he has done.

If it be worth the time, to sit as Master, and enjoy the honour, it is worth the trouble to keep the Company in the proud position in which it now is, for the Pattenmakers' Company is a household word amongst the City Companies, and the Master on leaving the Chair—(and returning his sincere thanks to those gentlemen who elected him to it, and to Richard Clout, Esq., who stood aside to let your Master take that high and onerous position)—trusts that those who follow him will do their best to preserve the Company in the same state as he now leaves it.

The Master commits the Company to your charge with the full conviction that each in his vocation will follow in the steps of those who have gone before him. Need he point out the Grand Banquets and Hospitality, the Visitors, &c., who were invited under the rule of Barrow Emanuel, Esq., of the late C. W. Thompson, Esq., of our lamented friend and Master, Mr. Taylor, and others, who had gone before him, and in whose shoes he has

endeavoured to tread. And with these words he bids
you farewell as Master, yet with the fullest inten-
tions to back up each succeeding Master, with such
help as your retiring Master can give ; and that
the Worshipful Company of Pattenmakers may
flourish, root and branch, and continue for ever,
notwithstanding the blasts of political opinion, is
the best wish of your retiring Master, and may
the Almighty bless each and all of you, is the
prayer of your Sincere Friend,

GEORGE LAMBERT, F.S.A.,
Major 13th Middlesex.

LONDON:
T. BRETTELL AND CO. PRINTERS,
RUPERT ST., HAYMARKET, W.

www.ingramcontent.com/pod-product-compliance
Lightning Source LLC
Chambersburg PA
CBHW021640270326
41931CB00008B/1095